The Power of the Cross

DISCOVERY SERIES BIBLE STUDY

For individuals or groups

We see power all around us—symbolized in so many ways. We look at a nation's capital and see the immense power of government. We look at a place like Wall Street and see the power of money. But where is the real power in our world?

Surprisingly, to find that answer we have to travel back in time—two millennia to be exact—to a darkened hill outside Jerusalem. There we see what looks like a powerless man being inhumanely killed on a crude cross in the worst case of judicial injustice of all time.

What we don't see in that gruesome scene is that the One hanging on that cross will soon display His power in ways that still hold us in awe. In just a matter of days, this man will come alive again—and we will begin to understand the significance of this event. Join **Bill Crowder** as he unfolds for us the immense power of Jesus' cross.

This Discovery Series Bible Study is based on *The Power of the Cross* (HP131), one of the popular Discovery Series booklets from Our Daily Bread Ministries. Find out more about Discovery Series at discoveryseries.org

Discovery House is affiliated with Our Daily Bread Ministries, Grand Rapids, Michigan.

Requests for permission to quote from this book should be directed to: Permissions Department, Discovery House, PO Box 3566, Grand Rapids, MI 49501, or contact us by e-mail at permissionsdept@dhp.org

Managing Editor: Dave Branon
Study Guide questions: Dave Branon
Graphic Design: Steve Gier

COVER PHOTO:
Ole Kristen Johansen via Stockvault.com

INSIDE PHOTOS:
Courtesy of The Walters Art Museum, painting by Gerbrand van den Eeckhout (public domain), p.6; Spanish Browne via FreeImages.com, p.10; Adrian van Leen via RGBStock.com, p.12; François-André Vincent (public domain), p.13; The British Museum (public domain), p.16; Michaela Kobyakov via RGBStock.com (composite), p.18; Paolo Veronese (public domain), p.19; Frederick Wellington Ruckstuhl (public domain), p.24; Robert Linder via RGBStock.com, p.26; Gustave Doré (public domain), p.27; Peter Paul Rubens (public domain), p.32; Terry Bidgood, p.34; The brothers Albermann (public domain), p.35; Gustave Doré (public domain), p.40; Frank Becker via Pixabay.com, p.42

ISBN: 978-1-62707-338-7
Printed in the United States of America
First Printing in 2015

Table of Contents

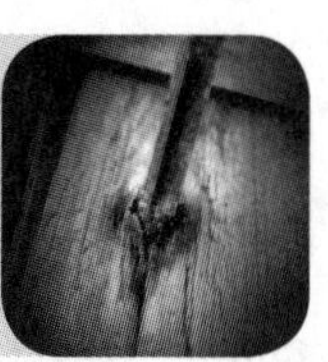

How To Use
DISCOVERY SERIES BIBLE STUDIES

The Purpose

The Discovery Series Bible Study (DSBS) series provides assistance to pastors and lay leaders in guiding and teaching fellow Christians with lessons adapted from Discovery Series booklets from Our Daily Bread Ministries and supplemented with items taken from the pages of *Our Daily Bread.* The DSBS series uses the inductive study method to help Christians understand the Bible more clearly.

The Format

READ: Each DSBS book is divided into a series of lessons. For each lesson, you will read a few pages that will give you insight into one aspect of the overall study. Included in some studies will be FOCAL POINT and TIME OUT FOR THEOLOGY segments to help you think through the material. These can be used as discussion starters for group sessions.

RESPOND: At the end of the reading is a two-page STUDY GUIDE to help participants respond to and reflect on the subject. If you are the leader of a group study, ask each member to preview the STUDY GUIDE before the group gets together. Don't feel that you have to work your way through each question in the STUDY GUIDE; let the interest level of the participants dictate the flow of the discussion. The questions are designed for either group or individual study. Here are the parts of that guide:

MEMORY VERSE: A short Scripture passage that focuses your thinking on the biblical truth at hand and can be used for memorization. You might suggest memorization as a part of each meeting.

WARMING UP: A general interest question that can foster discussion (group) or contemplation (individual).

THINKING THROUGH: Questions that will help a group or a student interact with the reading. These questions help drive home the critical concepts of the book.

DIGGING IN: An inductive study of a related passage of Scripture, reminding the group or the student of the importance of Scripture as the final authority.

GOING FURTHER: A two-part wrap-up of the response: REFER suggests ways to compare the ideas of the lesson with teachings in other parts of the Bible. REFLECT challenges the group or the learner to apply the teaching in real life.

OUR DAILY BREAD: After each STUDY GUIDE session will be an *Our Daily Bread* article that relates to the topic. You can use this for further reflection or for an introduction to a time of prayer.

Go to the Leader's and User's Guide on page 43 for further suggestions about using this Discovery Series Bible Study.

1

INTRODUCTION

THE Life OF One Soldier

When I wrote the book *Windows on Easter,* from which this study guide is adapted, my goal was to take a fresh look at the familiar events of the death and resurrection of Christ by seeing them through the eyes of some of the men and women who were there. Those moments that opened eternity for the undeserving at the cost of the life of the One who is eternally worthy must never be allowed to grow stale.

One of the eyewitnesses was the **Roman centurion** who assisted at the crucifixion itself. The old spiritual asks the haunting question: "Were you there when they crucified MY Lord?"

Oh, yes. This man was there!

As we try to imagine what he saw and felt, may the grace and mercy of Christ grasp our hearts in a way that transforms us deeply, just as the centurion was transformed.

Through the centuries, soldiers have been both despised and revered—despised by those they attack and conquer but revered and honored by those they protect and defend. We are often shocked by the actions that war, itself a result of hatred and sin, compels military personnel to take; yet we are frequently amazed by the courage it requires for soldiers to take those actions.

Even hearts hardened by the heat of battles and the struggles of military service are not beyond the reach of the gospel or the power of the cross.

Those of us who have never experienced the horror of combat cannot comprehend the toll a soldier's work takes on him or her. Although we can't fully understand, we appreciate the significant sacrifices soldiers make and what they have endured in the line of duty.

Endured? Yes, that is the right word. The soldier's task is far from easy and often extremely unpleasant. Soldiers suffer the hardships of training and are often subjected, in duty or in combat, to a lifestyle of

> Through the centuries, soldiers have been despised and they have been revered—despised by those they attack and conquer, revered by those they protect and defend.

deprivation. It is a life that sometimes seems barely civilized, alternating between acts of valor and barbarism. The soldier's life is also an existence filled with danger—especially because many times the soldier doesn't know where danger is coming from.

The story is told of an order sent at the outbreak of World War I from headquarters in London to a British outpost in Africa. The order read, "We are at war. Arrest all foreigners." A short time later, the outpost sent the following response to HQ: "We have arrested ten Germans, six Belgians, four Frenchmen, two Italians, three Austrians, and an American. Please advise immediately who we're at war with." While humorous, that story nevertheless reminds us that part of the terror of war is its unpredictability. And that is a fearful thing, indeed.

There is a another frightening aspect to life as a soldier, however, and that is the constant reality of being faced with death; this reality often leads to what is known as "foxhole prayers—desperate pleas to God, even from soldiers who aren't always convinced God is there. To live continually in the shadow of death, to face the reality that you are agent of death—even for a just cause—is a difficult thing, to say the least. Being forced to take another's life, even during a war

> "Endure hardship as a good soldier of Jesus Christ."
> 2 TIMOTHY 2:3

that is considered justifiable, can be extremely hard to live with.

The life of a soldier is not an easy life. It isn't now, and it wasn't two thousand years ago.

Yet, even hearts hardened by the heat of battles and the struggles of military service are not beyond the reach of the gospel or the power of the cross. In fact, no person is stronger than the power of the cross.

The soldier's life is an existence filled with danger.

Let's look at this power at work in the life of one soldier, a person of significance who, in turn, declared the significance of the Christ. The soldier in question? The centurion in charge of the crucifixion of Jesus Christ.

1 The Life of One Soldier

STUDY GUIDE

read pages 6–9

To begin to think about the challenges and sacrifices of being a soldier.

MEMORY VERSE
Acts 10:1—
"There was a certain man in Caesarea called Cornelius, a centurion."

Warming Up

Do you know someone who is active in the military—or were you ever in the service? In brief, what stood out as characteristic of being a soldier?

Thinking Through

1. Have you ever thought seriously about the question of the song mentioned: "Were you there when they crucified my Lord?" What do you think would have touched your heart the most if you had been there?

2. Think as well about the soldiers who were there. This was their job—to monitor the ones being crucified. What might have they been thinking?

3. Bill Crowder mentions "foxhole prayers." Have you ever been in a situation when you sent that kind of emergency prayer God's way? What was the situation?

Going Further

Refer

The Old Testament mentions great numbers of soldiers in some of the conflicts in ancient times. Notice the vast armies in these passages:

1 Samuel 4:10

2 Kings 13:7

1 Chronicles 18:4

Digging In — Read 2 Timothy 2:1–4

You therefore, my son, be strong
in the grace that is in Christ Jesus.
2 And the things that you have heard
from me among many witnesses,
commit these to faithful men who
will be able to teach others also.
3 You therefore must endure hardship as a good soldier of Jesus
Christ. 4 No one engaged in warfare
entangles himself with the affairs of
this life, that he may please him
who enlisted him as a soldier.

1. According to 2 Timothy 2:3, followers of Jesus must "endure hardship as a good soldier of Jesus Christ." What do we see in verses 1 and 2 that suggest what that means we should do?

2. A good soldier, according to verse 4, does not entangle himself in the affairs of this life. What does that mean?

3. We as people redeemed by Jesus have been "enlisted" by Jesus. What happens with a real soldier, such as the centurion at the cross, when he becomes "enlisted" by both his field of service and by Jesus? Was there tension for someone like the centurion when he turned to Jesus?

Prayer Time

Use the *Our Daily Bread* article on the next page as a guide for reflection on soldiers and centurions.

Reflect

1. When we trusted Jesus, we enlisted in His army as His soldiers. What should that mean to us?

2. Do you know any good soldiers in Jesus' army who are also good soldiers for their country's military? What can we learn from that dual allegiance?

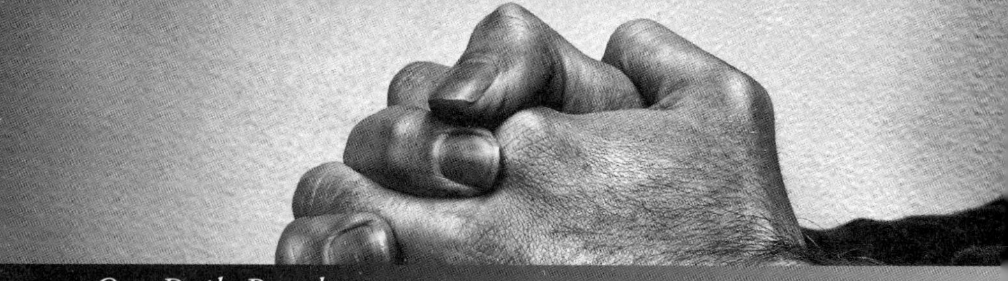

Our Daily Bread: For reflection about **soldiers and centurions**

Foxhole Prayers

"Foxhole prayers" come from soldiers who ordinarily give little or no thought to God but who cry out to Him when they are under heavy enemy attack. Crouching in their trenches, they plead in desperation for their lives. They are not the only ones to offer foxhole prayers, though. The only time many people pray is when they're afraid and in trouble.

Two small boys were talking about prayer. One asked the other if his family prayed together in the morning. "No," came the reply, "my mother has me say my prayers only when I go to bed and it's dark. I guess there's nothing to be afraid of when it's light."

We need not be ashamed of calling on the Lord in times of danger and fear. But our prayers should be just as frequent and natural "when it's light" as "when it's dark." Hannah exemplified this. Greatly disappointed because she was childless, she "was in bitterness of soul . . . and wept in anguish." In that state she rightly "prayed to the LORD" (1 SAMUEL 1:10). Later, in 1 Samuel 2, however, she can also be heard praying after the darkness had gone and she was rejoicing in the sunlight of God's favor.

We should pray in our "foxholes," but that's not the only time. We should also pray when all is well. In fact, we should "pray without ceasing."

—Richard DeHaan

1 THESS. 5:17—
Pray without ceasing.

Read today's *Our Daily Bread* at **odb.org**

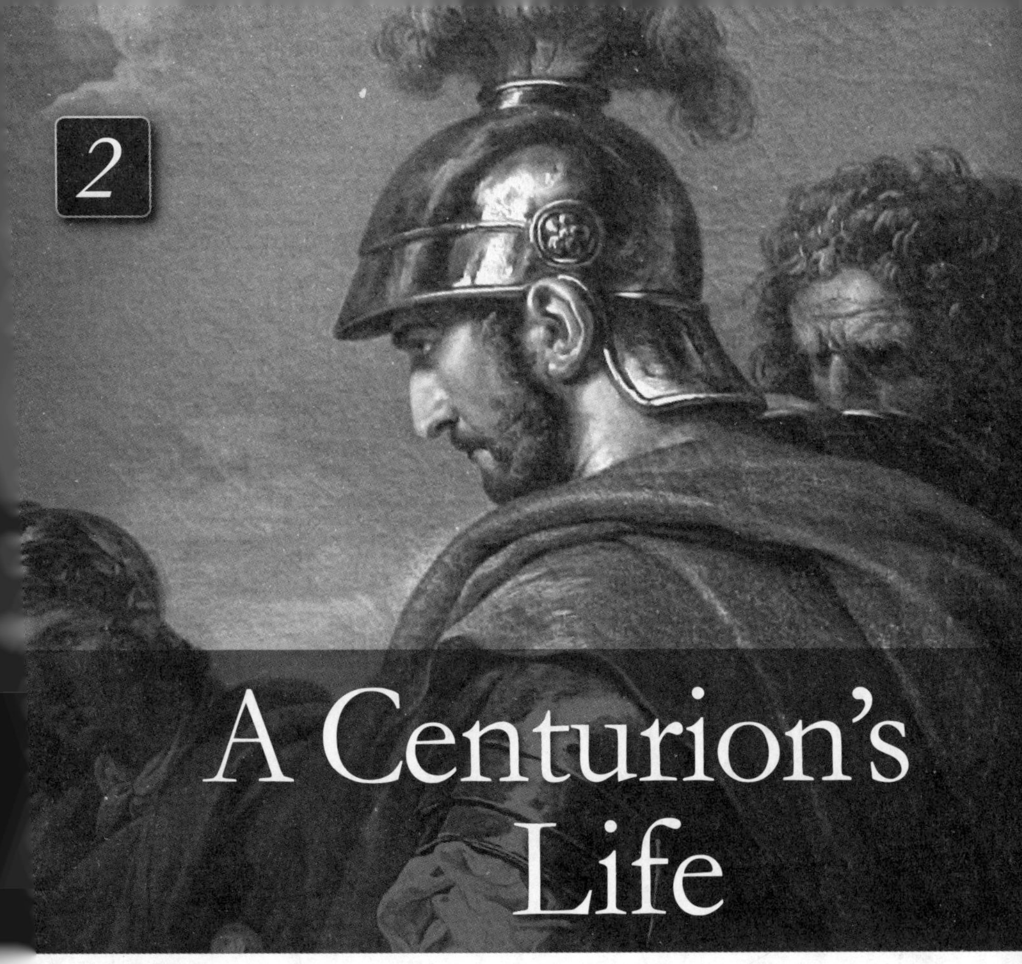

2 A Centurion's Life

Our eldest son has been in the Army for several years. Watching him progress through the ranks from recruit to staff sergeant has been an education in what military life is like. Soldiers are committed to putting the mission before comfort, their comrades before self, and obedience to duty above their personal opinions about the orders they are given. It is a lifestyle rooted in discipline, authority structures, and teamwork.

The core elements of soldiering have not changed over the centuries. Certainly the technology, the apparatus of warfare, and the

FOCAL POINT

Centurions were professional soldiers exerting the iron heel of Rome . . . Yet the centurions mentioned in the New Testament are uniformly spoken of in terms of praise.

training have changed. But the basic commitments to obedience, duty, discipline, authority, and teamwork have not. So with that in mind, let's consider what military life might have looked like for a first-century Roman centurion.

The word *centurion* comes from the Latin term *centum* meaning "one hundred." A centurion was a Roman officer in command of a hundred men. To have a proper grasp of a centurion's role, it is helpful to understand the design of a Roman legion.

Each legion was divided into ten cohorts, each cohort into three maniples, and each maniple into two centuries. In a legion there were thirty maniples and sixty centuries. A century always consisted of a hundred soldiers, meaning that sixty centuries formed a combined legion of six thousand troops.

In the Roman army, the office of centurion was the highest rank an ordinary soldier could achieve. The position was similar to what we know as a company commander. Sixty centurions served each legion, with rankings among those sixty. Promotion to the office of centurion was usually based on experience and knowledge, and—just as with officers in the military today—centurions were promoted as they transferred to positions of increasing responsibility.

The centurion typically earned his rank the hard way, and it was a position of prestige and honor, commanding the respect of others. Centurions received substantial pensions at retirement and were viewed as notables in the towns where they lived. The centurions mentioned in Luke 7 and Acts 10 were men of financial means who contributed to their communities and were respected.

It was not easy to gain the strategic position of centurion. While it is true that some were able to purchase their rank and some were appointed because they were favored by higher ranking officers or Roman officials, most centurions were appointed by the tribunes over them. These promotions were almost always based on a soldier's merit, with good conduct being a key consideration.

A centurion's tasks fell into two basic areas. In combat, he was responsible for implementing military strategy. He would almost always be on point, leading the charge into battle. Away from the battlefield, the centurion administered discipline in the ranks, mediated interpersonal conflicts among his men, provided security and protection when called upon, supervised police actions in occupied areas, and, most notably for our purposes, oversaw executions. As a general rule, these executions were done for the sword for Roman citizens (Romans 13) and by crucifixion by non-Romans (*Harper's Bible Dictionary*).

FOCAL POINT

Crucifixion was a method of execution commonly practiced by the Roman Empire. It probably originated in ancient Persia and was adopted by Alexander the Great. The crucified victim was tied or nailed to a large, wooden T-shaped cross and left to hang until dead.

2 A Centurion's Life

STUDY GUIDE
read pages 13–15

MEMORY VERSE
Luke 7:2—

"A certain centurion's servant, who was dear to him, was sick and ready to die."

To become familiar with the life and work of centurions.

Warming Up

Do you know someone or was anyone in your group ever an officer in the armed forces? What stood out about that person's leadership and demeanor?

Thinking Through

1. The text of this section says that a centurion was in charge of one hundred soldiers. What kinds of difficulties might come up while making sure so many soldiers worked and lived together as a unit?

2. "Centurions . . . were viewed as notables in the towns where they lived." Is that true today of officers in the armed forces after they retire?

3. At the end of this session, we get to the item that is most relevant to this study. Centurions "oversaw executions." What does it mean to you to hear Jesus' crucifixion labeled as an execution—given what we know about that term today?

Going Further

Refer

Read about the centurion in Matthew 8. How does this soften your impression of a leader with great authority?

Digging In Read Luke 7:1–10

1. What does it tell you about the centurion that he had a servant? And what does it tell you about him that he "sent elders of the Jews" to Jesus with his request?

2. What do we find out about the centurion in the Jewish elders' plea to Jesus (vv. 4–5)?

3. Finally, what do we discover about this centurion when he begins to talk with Jesus (vv. 6–8)?

Now when [Jesus] concluded all
His sayings in the hearing of the
people, He entered Capernaum.
2 And a certain centurion's servant,
who was dear to him, was sick and
ready to die. 3 So when he heard
about Jesus, he sent elders of the Jews
to Him, pleading with Him to come
and heal his servant. 4 And when they
came to Jesus, they begged Him ear-
nestly, saying that the one for whom
He should do this was deserving,
5 "for he loves our nation, and has
built us a synagogue." 6 Then Jesus
went with them. And when He was
already not far from the house, the
centurion sent friends to Him, saying
to Him, "Lord, do not trouble
Yourself, for I am not worthy that
You should enter under my roof.
7 Therefore I did not even think
myself worthy to come to You. But
say the word, and my servant will be
healed. 8 For I also am a man placed
under authority, having soldiers
under me. And I say to one, 'Go,' and
he goes; and to another, 'Come,' and
he comes; and to my servant, 'Do
this,' and he does it."
9 When Jesus heard these things, He
marveled at him, and . . . said to the
crowd that followed Him, "I say to you,
I have not found such great faith, not
even in Israel!" 10 And those who were
sent, returning to the house, found the
servant well who had been sick.

Prayer Time

Use the *Our Daily Bread* article on the next page as a guide for reflection on soldiers and centurions.

Reflect

1. There is a lesson here for any of us who might be in a position of leadership. What about the centurion makes you respect him?

2. What would it take for us to earn the right to hear Jesus say of us: "I have not found such great faith"?

Unanswered Prayers

An explanation we often hear for "unanswered" prayers is that we don't have enough faith. But Jesus said in Luke 17:6 that if we have faith the size of a mustard seed, we can command a mulberry tree to be uprooted and planted in the sea and it will obey us. In other words, the effectiveness of our prayers depends not on how much faith we have but on whether we even have faith.

Luke tells of a Roman centurion with "great faith" (7:9). His faith was expressed first as an appeal to Jesus to heal his dying servant. Then it was expressed as an acknowledgment that Jesus could heal his servant anytime, anywhere. The centurion did not ask Jesus to do things his way.

Faith has been described as "trusting God's heart and trusting God's power." Some prayers that seem to go unanswered are simply instances in which God has lovingly overruled our wishes. He knows that what we have asked for is not best. Or it may be that our timing is not His timing, or He has some far greater purpose in mind. Let us remember, even Jesus prayed to His heavenly Father, "Nevertheless not My will, but Yours" (LUKE 22:42).

Do we have the centurion's great faith—a faith that trusts God to do His work in His way?

—C. P. Hia

LUKE 7:9—

[Jesus said], "I have not found such great faith, not even in Israel!"

Read today's *Our Daily Bread* at **odb.org**

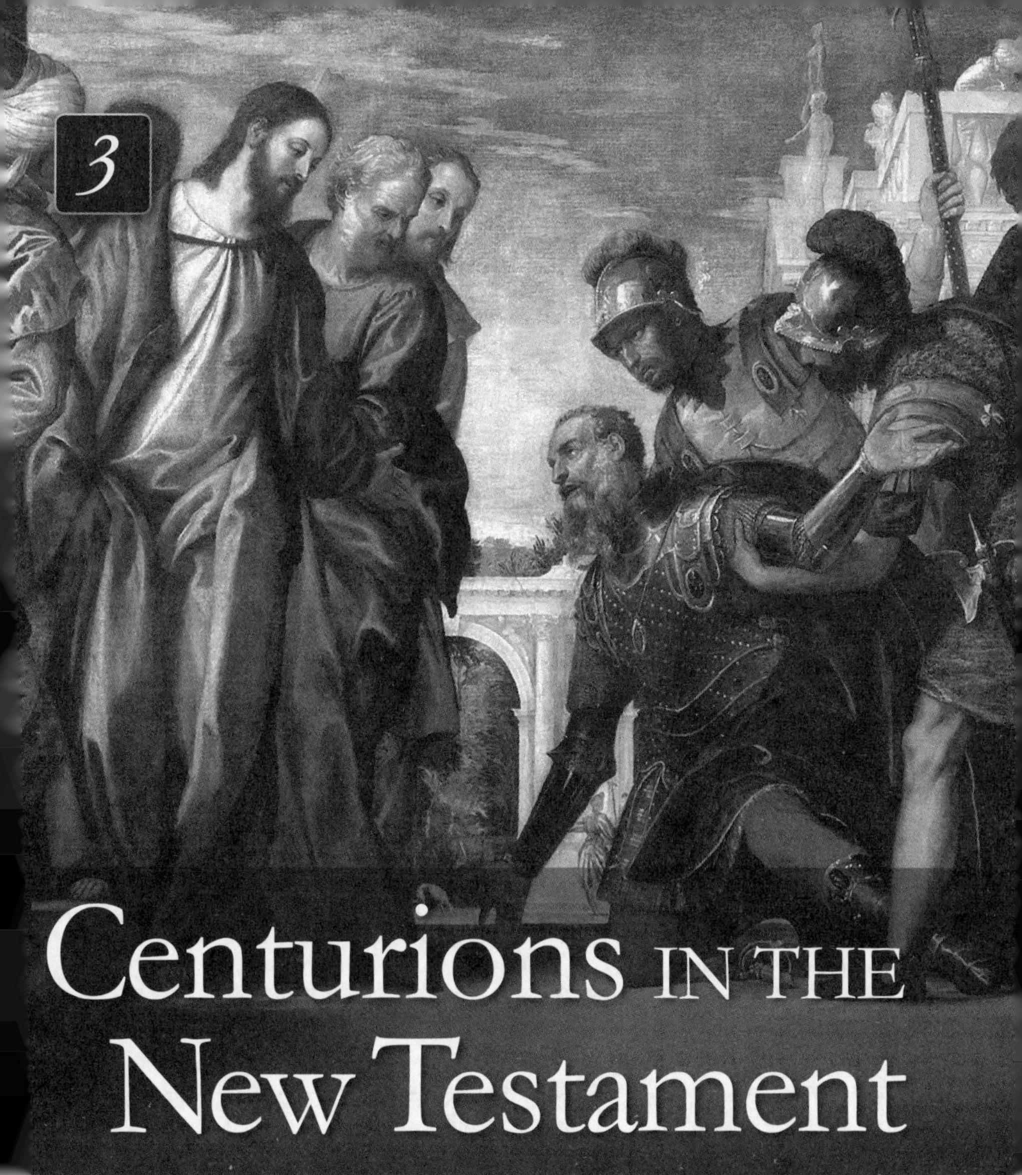

3

Centurions IN THE New Testament

Several centurions are mentioned in the New Testament. The accounts of the more prominent ones reveal the degree to which Christ's message and influence were crossing social, ethnic, and political lines and barriers.

The Centurion of Capernaum (Matthew 8:5–13)

Now when Jesus had entered Capernaum, a centurion came to Him, pleading with Him, saying, "Lord, my servant is lying at home paralyzed, dreadfully tormented." And Jesus said to him, "I will come and heal him." The centurion answered and said, "Lord, I am not worthy that You should come under my roof. But only speak a word, and my servant will be healed. For I also am a man under authority, having soldiers under me. And I say to this one, 'Go,' and he goes; and to another, 'Come,' and he comes; and to my servant, 'Do this,' and he does it." When Jesus heard it, He marveled, and said this to those who followed, "Assuredly, I say to you, I have not found such great faith, not even in Israel! And I say to you that many will come from east and west, and sit down with Abraham, Isaac, and Jacob in the kingdom of heaven. But the sons of the kingdom will be cast out into outer darkness. There will be weeping and gnashing of teeth." Then Jesus said to the centurion, "Go your way; and as you have believed, so let it be done for you." And his servant was healed that same hour.

This man came to Jesus on behalf of his servant. He exhibited great submission (calling Jesus "Lord") and great faith in declaring that he believed that Christ need only say the word and his servant would be made whole. As if this weren't

FOCAL POINT

In its first-century context, this scene is remarkable. First, a Roman centurion calling a Jewish rabbi "Lord," shows submission to a Jewish teacher. Second, Jesus' action, going into a Gentile's home, would have immediately rendered Him ceremonially unclean—making it impossible for Him to participate in temple worship. This interaction shows great love and deference by each man toward the other.

> This encounter makes it clear that neither ethnic background nor vocation determines one's fitness for kingdom citizenship.

remarkable enough, this man gives us the unusual picture of the conquering warrior showing deep concern for a mere slave. To show such deep concern that he would seek out the Rabbi of Nazareth for help is truly amazing.

The Centurion of Caesarea (Acts 10:1–2, 22, 44–48)

There was a certain man in Caesarea called Cornelius, a centurion of what was called the Italian Regiment, a devout man and one who feared God with all his household, who gave alms generously to the people, and prayed to God always. . . .

And they said [to Peter], "Cornelius the centurion, a just man, one who fears God and has a good reputation among all the nation of the Jews, was divinely instructed by a holy angel to summon you to his house, and to hear words from you." . . .

While Peter was still speaking these words, the Holy Spirit fell upon all those who heard the word. And those of the circumcision who believed were astonished, as many as came with Peter, because the gift of the Holy Spirit had been poured out on the Gentiles also. . . . Then Peter answered, "Can anyone forbid water, that these should not be baptized who have received the Holy Spirit just as we have?" And he commanded them to be baptized in the name of the Lord. Then they asked him to stay a few days.

Cornelius, a prominent Gentile convert, was a centurion who had dealt kindly with and was appreciated by the Jewish people. Through his exposure to Judaism, his heart had been prepared for the seed of the gospel, and when Peter came to him with the message of the cross, he believed.

The Centurion of the Shipwreck (Acts 27:1, 11, 42–44; 28:16)

And when it was decided that we should sail to Italy, they delivered Paul and some other prisoners to one named Julius, a centurion of the Augustan Regiment. . . .

Nevertheless the centurion was more persuaded by the helmsman and the owner of the ship than by the things spoken by Paul. . . .

And the soldiers' plan was to kill the prisoners, lest any of them should swim away and escape. But the centurion, wanting to save Paul, kept them from their purpose, and commanded that those who could swim should jump overboard first and get to land, and the rest, some on boards and some on parts of the ship. . . .

Now when we came to Rome, the centurion delivered the prisoners to the captain of the guard; but Paul was permitted to dwell by himself with the soldier who guarded him.

Julius, the centurion responsible for delivering Paul to Rome for trial, was reluctant to accept the apostle's counsel at first. During the shipwreck experience, however, he was exposed to the vitality of Paul's faith and saw the power of God in the miraculous. He saved Paul's life when it was threatened.

Centurions were not the ancient equivalent of "the boy next door." They were part of an occupation force—professional soldiers exerting the iron heel of Rome and its subjugation and bondage. They represented everything that the Jews of the first century hated, yet, in spite of all that, one writer ob-

> The accounts of more prominent centurions reveal the degree to which Christ's message and influence were crossing social, ethnic, and political lines and barriers.

served, "The centurions mentioned in the New Testament were uniformly spoken of in terms of praise, whether in the Gospels or in the Acts" (*Easton's Bible Dictionary*).

That seems counterintuitive and is certainly unexpected. Perhaps these consistent descriptions are rooted in the evidence of their character. Roman historian Polybius noted a fact of great significance: Centurions were chosen by merit and were remarkable not so much for their daring courage and valor (although those qualities were important) as for their deliberation, constancy, and strength of mind.

Bible scholar William Barclay quoted Polybius regarding centurions:

> *They must not be much venturesome seekers after danger as men who can command, steady in action and reliable; they ought not to be overanxious to rush into the fight, but when hard-pressed they must be ready to hold their ground and die at their posts.*

Barclay, faced with the evidence, concluded, "The centurions were the finest men in the Roman army."

This historical background sets the stage for the appearance of the centurion at the cross and for the weight and the credibility of his words.

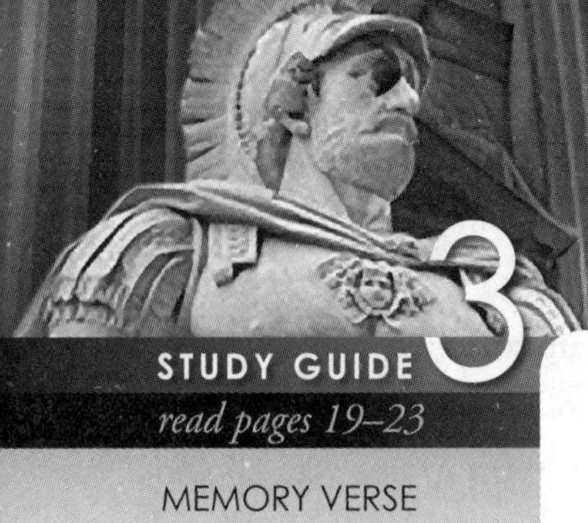

3 Centurions in the New Testament

STUDY GUIDE

read pages 19–23

To see, by looking at New Testament centurions, how the gospel crosses various barriers.

MEMORY VERSE
Matthew 8:8 —

"Lord, I am not worthy that You should come under my roof."

Warming Up

Who are your favorite "war heroes"? What stands out about their stories?

Thinking Through

1. What does it tell us about the centurion at Capernaum that he (a) cared so much for his servant and (b) called on Jesus to help him?

2. Bill Crowder says, "Through his exposure to Judaism, [Cornelius'] heart had been prepared for the seed of the gospel" (page 21). What does that help us understand about witnessing to people of a different faith background?

3. What surprises you about the actions of the centurion named Julius in Paul's shipwreck story?

Going Further

Refer

There are 25 verses that refer to centurions in the New Testament. Go to **Biblegateway.com** or a concordance, find some of those verses, and seek out three characteristics of the centurions presented in those verses.

Digging In — Read Matthew 8:5–13

1. From the context clues in Matthew 8:5–6, what can you tell about how this Capernaum centurion felt about his servant?

2. What was the centurion indicating to Jesus when he said, "For I also am a man under authority, having soldiers under me" (v. 9)?

3. What promise did Jesus make to the centurion in verse 13?

5 Now when Jesus had entered
Capernaum, a centurion came to
Him, pleading with Him, 6 saying,
"Lord, my servant is lying at home
paralyzed, dreadfully tormented."
7 And Jesus said to him, "I will
come and heal him."
8 The centurion answered and said,
"Lord, I am not worthy that You
should come under my roof. But
only speak a word, and my servant
will be healed. 9 For I also am a man
under authority, having soldiers
under me. And I say to this one,
'Go,' and he goes; and to another,
'Come,' and he comes; and to my
servant, 'Do this,' and he does it."
10 When Jesus heard it, He marveled,
and said to those who followed,
"Assuredly, I say to you, I have not
found such great faith, not even in
Israel! 11 And I say to you that many
will come from east and west, and
sit down with Abraham, Isaac, and
Jacob in the kingdom of heaven.
12 But the sons of the kingdom will
be cast out into outer darkness.
There will be weeping and gnashing
of teeth." 13 Then Jesus said to the
centurion, "Go your way; and as
you have believed, so let it be done
for you." And his servant was healed
that same hour.

Prayer Time

Use the *Our Daily Bread* article on the next page as a guide for reflection on soldiers and centurions.

Reflect

1. Centurions were tough, strong men accustomed to doing difficult tasks and carrying out tough orders. Yet the centurions Jesus and Paul encountered showed kindness and compassion. What does that say about manliness and its relation to the gospel?

2. Have you ever put up a manmade barrier between yourself and another person—just because of perception? How does this study help you see how wrong that is?

Under Authority

In answer to a Roman centurion's earnest plea to heal his desperately ill slave, Jesus started to go to the man's house. The man, however, said that he was unworthy of such attention. He said, "Only speak a word, and my servant will be healed. For I also am a man under authority, having soldiers under me" (MATTHEW 8:8–9). If he, an officer in the Roman army, could have things done by a word of command, surely Jesus, the great prophet of God, could do likewise.

A centurion had one hundred men under his command. Above him was the senior centurion, and above the senior centurion, the sixty centurions of the Roman legion. Above the sixty centurions were the six tribunes, and above the six tribunes the two consuls. Above the two consuls was the emperor himself. It was because the Roman centurion stood in this long line of delegated authority that he was able to give orders and have them obeyed. He had authority because he himself was under authority.

Today, those of us who submit to Christ are men and women "under authority." Because of our relationship to Him, we have the authority to speak on His behalf, declaring forgiveness of sins to all who believe in Him.

Do we live and speak as people under authority?

—Haddon Robinson

2 CORINTHIANS 5:20—

Now then, we are ambassadors for Christ, as though God were pleading through us: we implore you on Christ's behalf, be reconciled to God.

Read today's *Our Daily Bread* at **odb.org**

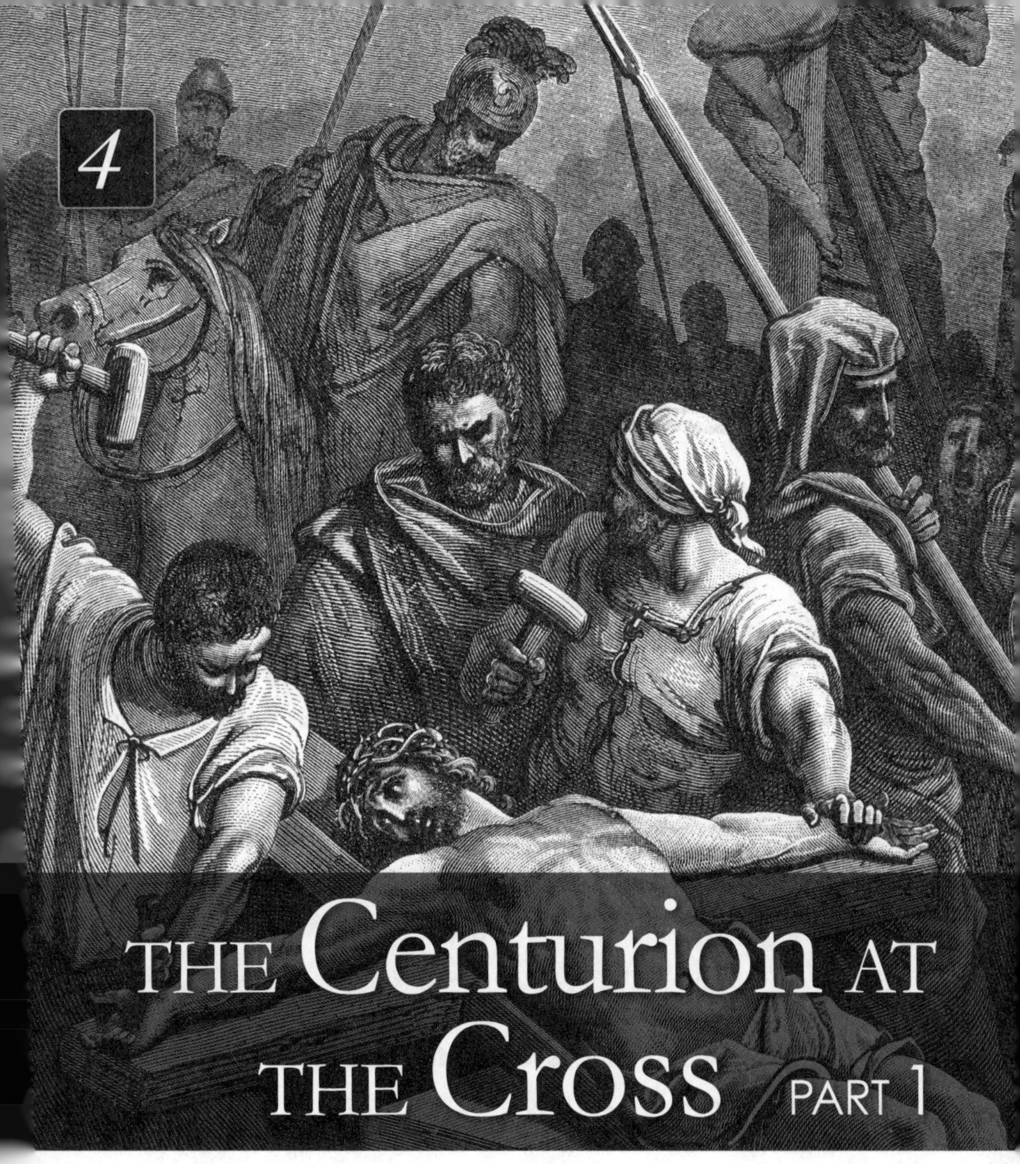

4

THE Centurion AT THE Cross PART 1

Now from the sixth hour until the ninth hour there was darkness over all the land. And about the ninth hour Jesus cried out with a loud voice, saying, "Eli, Eli, lama sabachthani?" that is, "My God, My God, why have You forsaken Me?"…

And Jesus cried out again with a loud voice, and yielded up His spirit.

Then, behold, the veil of the temple was torn in two from top to bottom; and the earth quaked, and the rocks were split, and the graves were opened; and many bodies of the saints who had fallen asleep were raised; and coming out of the graves after His resurrection, they went into the holy city and appeared to many.

So when the centurion and those with him, who were guarding Jesus, saw the earthquake and the things that had happened, they feared greatly, saying, "Truly this was the Son of God!" (MATTHEW 27:45–46, 50–54).

"Truly this was the Son of God!" What a declaration! These were not quavering words from a frightened pup of a recruit or an easily manipulated conscript. This was the reasoned observation of a seasoned veteran who had watched men die horrible deaths—and had been putting them to death—for years.

Some have speculated about what he meant—was this a confession of faith, or was he just trying to define something outside the scope of his experience? I believe the answer is in the context. Obviously the centurion was deeply moved by the events he had witnessed, and the declaration of deity is what followed his observation.

We need to consider two things in order to fully and carefully consider the magnitude of the centurion's words: the evidence against this declaration and the evidence in support of this declaration.

The evidence against such a declaration was strong indeed. This centurion was well aware of the strong condemnation of the Jewish religious leaders that had put Jesus on the cross for making the claim to be the Son of God. His commander-in-chief, Pontius Pilate, had upheld the conviction for Jesus' making that claim. But the centurion rejects the condemnation and affirms Jesus' claim. Why? Because the arguments in favor of Christ's claim were overwhelming.

Looking at the evidence in support of this declaration, we must remember that this man had no doubt supervised many crucifixions. Yet there was something extraordinarily different about this particular execution.

> "Truly this was the Son of God!" These were not quavering words from a frightened pup of a recruit or an easily manipulated conscript.

What did he see? There are several scenes from the events of the arrest, trial, and crucifixion of Jesus that combine into a compelling mosaic.

- The **RESPONSE** of Jesus to the injustice that He had been forced to endure at the hands of His own countrymen through arrest and trials:

And while He was still speaking, behold, Judas, one of the twelve, with a great multitude with swords and clubs, came from the chief priests and elders of the people. Now His betrayer had given them a sign, saying, "Whomever I kiss, He is the One; seize Him." ... But Jesus said to him, "... How then could the Scriptures be fulfilled, that it must happen thus?" In that hour Jesus said to the multitudes, "Have you come out, as against a robber, with swords and clubs to take Me? I sat daily with you, teaching in the temple, and you did not seize Me. But all this was done that the Scriptures of the prophets might be fulfilled." Then all the disciples forsook Him and fled. ... And the high priest arose and said to Him, "Do You answer nothing? What is it these men testify against You?" But Jesus kept silent. And the high priest answered and said to Him, "I put You under oath by the living God: Tell us if you are the Christ, the Son of God!" Jesus said to him, "It is as you said. Nevertheless, I say to you, hereafter you will see the Son of Man sitting at the right hand of the Power, and coming on the clouds of heaven." Then the high priest tore his clothes, saying, "He has spoken blasphemy! What further need do we have of witnesses? Look, now you have heard His blasphemy! What do you think?" They answered and said, "He is deserving of death." Then they spat in His face and beat Him; and others struck Him with the palms of their hands, saying, "Prophesy to us, Christ! Who is the one who struck You?" (MATTHEW 26:47–68)

- The **RESPONSE** of Jesus to the torture that the centurion and his men had inflicted upon Him:

Then the soldiers of the governor took Jesus into the Praetorium and gathered the whole garrison around Him. And they stripped Him and put a scarlet robe on Him. When they had twisted a crown of thorns, they put it on His head, and a reed in His right hand. And they bowed the knee before Him and mocked Him, saying, "Hail, King of the Jews!" Then they spat on Him, and took the reed and struck Him on the head. And when they had mocked Him, they took the robe off Him, put his own clothes on Him, and led Him away to be crucified (27:27–31).

- The **DIGNITY** with which Jesus responded to the lynch mob that demanded His blood—as a sheep, silent before the slaughter. Scripture records no response by Jesus to the mob's cries:

But the chief priests stirred up the crowd, so that he should rather release Barabbas

FOCAL POINT

John 19:12–16: "From then on, Pilate sought to release Him, but the Jews cried out, saying, 'If you let this Man go, you are not Caesar's friend. Whoever makes himself a king speaks against Caesar.' . . . 'Away with Him, away with Him! Crucify Him!" Pilate said to them, 'Shall I crucify your King?' The chief priests answered, 'We have no king but Caesar!' Then [Pilate] delivered [Jesus] to them to be crucified."

First-century Jews expected a Messiah who would overthrow their oppressive Roman occupiers. Jesus, however, had come to overthrow the power and oppression of sin and death.

to them. Pilate answered and said to them again, "What then do you want me to do with Him whom you call the King of the Jews?" So they cried out again, "Crucify Him!" Then Pilate said to them, "Why, what evil has He done?" But they cried out all the more, "Crucify Him!" So Pilate, wanting to gratify the crowd, released Barabbas to them; and he delivered Jesus, after he had scourged Him, to be crucified (MARK 15:11–15 CF. ISAIAH 53:7).

• The **MERCY** of Jesus toward the people who rejected Him and the soldiers who crucified Him, including this centurion. His response? "Father, forgive them!" (LUKE 23:34). Even as they sat down to gamble (MATTHEW 27:35–36) for His meager possessions and to watch the gruesome spectacle, Jesus' concern was for their forgiveness, not His own escape. That is powerful!

• Creation's **RESPONSE** to the Creator's sin-bearing act. As Matthew records, witnesses "saw the earthquake and the things that [were happening]" (27:54). They saw the sun go dark, they felt the power of the earth quaking under their feet—and they saw these supernatural phenomena suddenly end when Jesus yielded up His spirit with a loud voice and died.

4 The Centurion at the Cross (PART 1)

STUDY GUIDE

read pages 27–31

To begin to see the power of the cross through the eyes of an important eyewitness.

MEMORY VERSE

Matthew 27:54—

"The centurion . . . saw the earthquake and the things that had happened . . . saying, 'Truly this was the son of God!' "

Warming Up

What element of the crucifixion breaks your heart the most as you think about what Jesus endured?

Thinking Through

1. Imagine standing with the centurion at the foot of the cross. He has undoubtedly seen dozens of crucifixions—including three this day. What was it about this one that made him make his declaration of deity?

2. Bill Crowder says, "This centurion was well aware of the strong condemnation of the Jewish religious leaders that had put Jesus on the cross for making the claim to be the Son of God" (p. 28). What personal implications could there be for the centurion in making his statement recorded in Matthew 27:54?

3. Think of the impact of Jesus' declaration from the cross: "Father, forgive them!" (Luke 12:34). Contrast that with what the centurion usually heard from people being crucified.

Going Further

Refer

Take a look at the three places in the Gospels where the centurion makes his declaration about Jesus. What differences do you see in the accounts as recorded in Matthew 27:45–54, Mark 15:33–39, and Luke 23:44–47?

Digging In Read Matthew 27:45-54

1. How would you characterize the atmosphere near the cross when Jesus—the second person of the eternal Godhead—"cried with a loud voice," "My God, My God, why have You forsaken Me" (vv. 45–47)?

2. What did the people mean when they said, "Let us see if Elijah will come to save Him" (v. 49)?

3. The great miracle of this weekend is going to be the resurrection, but what other unusual Good Friday events got the centurion's attention?

45 Now from the sixth hour until
the ninth hour there was darkness
over all the land. 46 And about the
ninth hour Jesus cried out with a loud
voice, saying, "Eli, Eli, lama sabachthani?" that is, "My God, My God,
why have You forsaken Me?"
47 Some of those who stood there,
when they heard that, said, "This Man
is calling for Elijah!" 48 Immediately
one of them ran and took a sponge,
filled it with sour wine and put it on a
reed, and offered it to Him to drink.
49 The rest said, "Let Him alone; let us
see if Elijah will come to save Him."
50 And Jesus cried out again with a
loud voice, and yielded up His spirit.
51 Then, behold, the veil of the temple was torn in two from top to bottom; and the earth quaked, and the
rocks were split, 52 and the graves were
opened; and many bodies of the saints
who had fallen asleep were raised; 53
and coming out of the graves after His
resurrection, they went into the holy
city and appeared to many.
54 So when the centurion and those
with him, who were guarding Jesus,
saw the earthquake and the things
that had happened, they feared
greatly, saying, "Truly this was the
Son of God!"

Prayer Time

Use the *Our Daily Bread* article on the next page as a guide for reflection on soldiers and centurions.

Reflect

1. As you reflect on the events at the cross, what new elements stand up to you and renew your faith?

2. What about Jesus makes you say, "Truly this was the son of God?"

Our Daily Bread: For reflection about **soldiers and centurions**

Meeting Jesus

When the centurion watched Christ, the living Word, die on the cross, he declared in fear and wonder, "Truly this was the Son of God." So today, many who read the written Word and trace the Savior's steps in the Gospels have come to the same conclusion.

Many years ago, two men were discussing the life of Jesus of Nazareth. One of them said, "I think an interesting romance could be written about Him." The other replied, "And you're just the man to write it. First, set forth the view that Christ is divine. Then tear down that idea and portray Jesus as He was—a man among men."

The advice was acted upon and the book was written. The person who listened to the suggestion was Lew Wallace, and the novel he wrote was *Ben-Hur*. In the process of his research, Wallace found himself confronted by the unique Man of the Scriptures. The more he studied Jesus' life and character, the more profoundly he was convinced that He was divine. Finally, like the centurion beside the cross, he proclaimed, 'Truly this was the Son of God.' "

Read the New Testament and encounter the Man of Galilee. You too will acknowledge that Jesus is indeed the only begotten Son of God. And you will want to get to know this Savior more and more each day.

—Henry Bosch

MATTHEW 27:54—
"Truly this was the Son of God!"

■ Read today's *Our Daily Bread* at **odb.org**

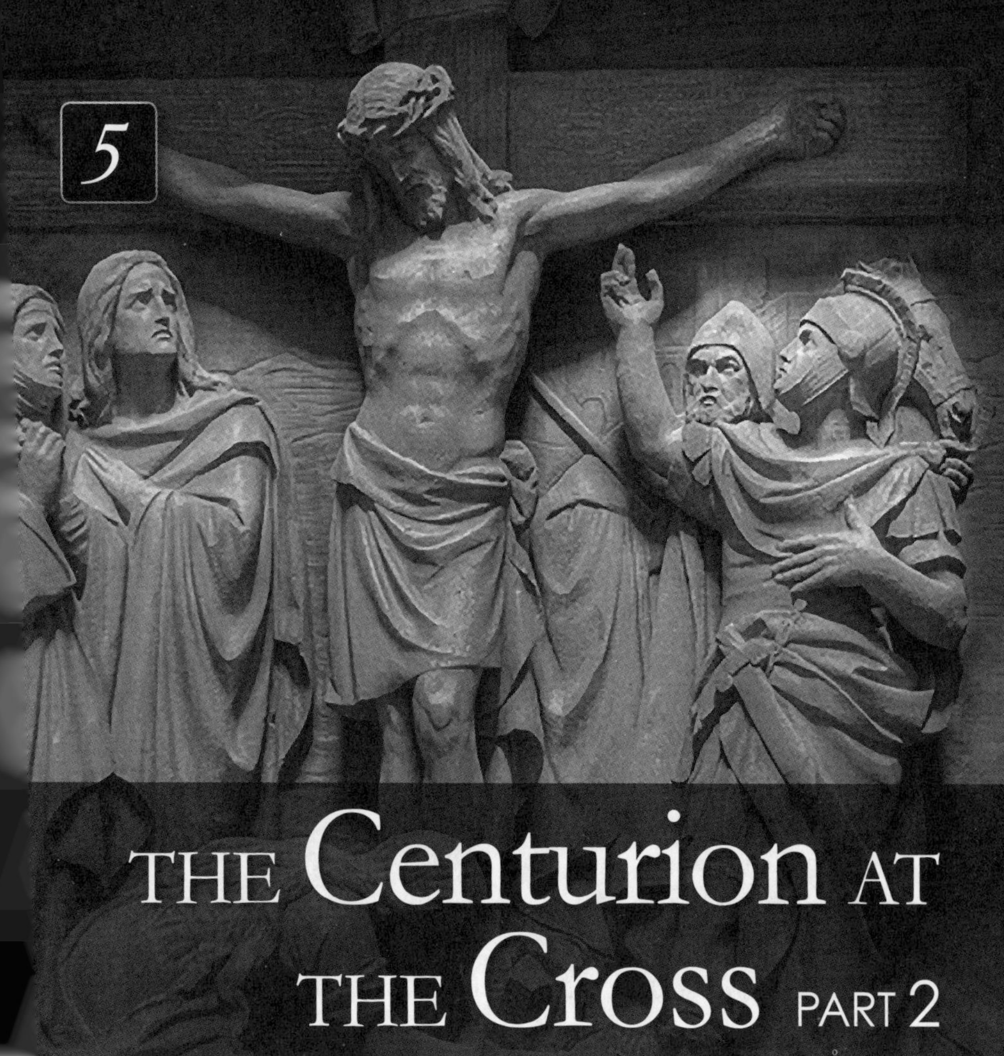

5

THE Centurion AT THE Cross PART 2

The centurion was understandably shocked by the significant events that accompanied the death of the Christ. In all of this up-close exposure to torture and death, he had never seen such things before, and the impact on him was inescapable.

> *There cannot be a reasonable doubt that this expression ["Truly this was the Son of God!"] was used in the Jewish sense, and that it points to the*

claim which Jesus made to be the Son of God, and on which His condemnation expressly turned. The meaning, then, clearly is that He must have been what He professed to be; in other words, that He was no impostor. There was no medium between those two (JAMIESON, FAUSSET, AND BROWN BIBLE COMMENTARY).

Bible scholar Dr. Herbert Lockyer writes, "What a remarkable testimony Christ received from this Gentile! How striking was the homage he paid to the crucified one at Golgotha!"

The centurion had seen, heard, and felt all the events of the crucifixion and death of Christ. As a result, he and his troops "became very frightened." The centurion and his group of battle-hardened soldiers had learned to cope with fear, but now they experienced sheer terror—not a true reverential fear, but perhaps, as commentator John Gill wrote, the "fear of punishment: lest divine vengeance should light on them for their concern in this matter."

> "What a remarkable testimony Christ received from this Gentile!"
>
> HERBERT LOCKYER

They had reason to be fearful because there was absolutely nothing ordinary about the significant events they were experiencing. It was:

• **No ordinary execution.** The darkness, the earthquake, and the cry of abandonment from Christ convinced the soldiers that this was no ordinary execution. The events terrified them and probably led them to believe that these things testified to heaven's wrath at the perpetuation of such a crime, in which they themselves had participated. What a realization! What a great fear to suddenly realize that you have put to death God's Son!

• **No ordinary power.** But there is more. They did not come to this conclusion because of the announcement of some angelic messenger or prophet.

Their conclusion came solely from the effects of the power of God on display at Calvary that dark day.

• **No ordinary confession.** The centurion's confession tells us something eternally important: Jesus as the promised Messiah and Son of God is seen most clearly in His passion and death. How interesting that the Jewish religious establishment had mocked Him with the title (V. 41–44) by which a Roman centurion now confessed Him.

Matthew Henry wrote: "The dreadful appearances of God in His providence sometimes work strangely for the conviction and awakening of sinners. This was expressed in the terror that fell upon the centurion and the Roman soldiers. Let us, with an eye of faith, behold Christ and Him crucified and be affected with that great love wherewith He loved us. Never were the horrid nature and effects of sin so tremendously displayed as on that day when the beloved son of the Father hung upon the Cross, suffering for sin, the Just for the unjust, that He might bring us to God. Let us yield ourselves willingly to His service."

Church tradition has given the name Petronius to this centurion. If he was won to faith in Christ, he came as a pagan and, like the thief on the cross who believed, was saved as Jesus hung upon the cross. How simple and basic is that? All who are ever saved in truth are saved because of the death of Jesus on the cross. So the cross began to do its work immediately. And that work has continued for two millennia.

The preaching of the cross may be foolishness to the world, but to those who are saved it is the power of God. No wonder Charles Wesley declared in

Jesus as the promised Messiah and Son of God is seen most clearly in His passion and death.

his anthem of praise for the death of Christ, "Amazing love, how can it be, that Thou, my God, shouldst die for me!"

It is that powerful cross and the love displayed there that moves hearts—even the hardened, battle-weary heart of a career soldier—from death to life.

The story is told of another soldier who also learned the significant lessons of Calvary. General Robert E. Lee, commander of the Confederate armies during America's Civil War, was attending a church service some time after the end of the war. At the conclusion of the sermon, Lee went forward to pray about things in his life that he had been convicted about during the message. As the general knelt praying, a former slave likewise stepped forward and knelt beside him—praying for his own spiritual needs. Once he had finished praying, Lee rose to leave and was stopped by a Southern former slave-owner who bemoaned the fact that a black man would be allowed to kneel beside Lee. The general, however, would have none of it and responded, "The ground is always level at the foot of the cross."

It was in the first century, and it still is today. The foot of the cross is where paupers and princes, religionists and pagans, well-knowns and unknowns, and—yes—generals and centurions find level ground to kneel and embrace the Christ who died for them—and for us.

The men and women who witnessed the trial, crucifixion, death, and resurrection of Christ saw more than words can ever express. They heard things that we can only imagine. But what they saw in their lifetime, we have seen in the Scriptures, and the result is amazingly the same. Though we may have not seen

> "And can it be that I should gain
> an interest in the Savior's blood?
> Died He for me, who caused His pain?
> For me, who Him to death pursued."
>
> CHARLES WESLEY

FOCAL POINT

It tells us something about the constant presence of the Roman army in Jesus day to consider that the word ***centurion*** is used 21 times in the gospels and in Acts.

Him physically, we have seen Him through the pages of Scripture and found solid ground for belief. The book of Romans explains the phenomenon this way: "So then faith comes by hearing, and hearing by the word of Christ" (10:17).

"Truly this was the Son of God!" We have heard and we have believed. But it must not end there. We must burn with the passion to know Him—the very passion of the apostle Paul, who wrote that his life's goal was "that I may know Him and the power of His resurrection, and the fellowship of His sufferings, being conformed to His death" (PHILIPPIANS 3:10).

May that same desire burn in our hearts as well, that we might truly know the One who loved us and gave himself for us.

5 The Centurion at the Cross (PART 2)

STUDY GUIDE

read pages 35–39

MEMORY VERSE

Luke 23:46-47—

"[Jesus] said, 'Father into Your hands I commit My spirit.' Having said this, He breathed His last. So when the centurion saw what happened, he glorified God."

To examine the ways the power of the cross had an impact on the centurion . . . and us.

Warming Up

When was a time in your life when you "feared greatly" as Matthew 27:54 says in describing the soldiers at the cross?

Thinking Through

1. An eyewitness to Jesus' crucifixion, according to the commentary quoted on page 36, decided that Jesus was "no impostor." Why is it hard for people today to agree with that discovery by the centurion?

2. Bill Crowder points out that the crucifixion demonstrated "no ordinary power." What were the specific examples of extraordinary power in the crucifixion passage?

3. We have not seen what the centurion saw; however, we believe in Jesus. What does that say about the power of the cross through the centuries?

Going Further

Refer

Notice what the following verses tell us about the power of the cross:

1 Corinthians 1:17–18

Galatians 6:14

Philippians 2:8

Hebrews 12:2

Digging In   Read Luke 23:44–48

1. We can only speculate about whether the centurion knew that the temple curtain had been torn in two (v. 45). What is the significance of that event in connection with the power of the cross?

2. The centurion's response was to glorify God (v. 47) because of the cross. How can we do the same thing today?

3. Compare "beat his breast" in Luke 18:13 and the same idea in Luke 23:48. What do you think this action meant at the cross?

44 Now it was about the sixth hour,
and there was darkness over all the
earth until the ninth hour. 45 Then
the sun was darkened, and the veil of
the temple was torn in two. 46 And
when Jesus had cried out with a loud
voice, He said, "Father, 'into Your
hands I commit My spirit.'" Having
said this, He breathed His last.
47 So when the centurion saw what
had happened, he glorified God, saying, "Certainly this was a righteous
Man!"
48 And the whole crowd who came
together to that sight, seeing what
had been done, beat their breasts
and returned.

Prayer Time

Use the *Our Daily Bread* article on the next page as a guide for reflection on soldiers and centurions.

Reflect

Think about all the ways the cross and its power have changed your life. Are there other people in your life who you think need to know about the power of the cross?

How can you reach out to them?

Our Daily Bread: For reflection about **soldiers and centurions**

The Cross Speaks

Crosses decorate church steeples and designate burial places. Sometimes they mark the spot where people died in highway accidents. And they are often worn as jewelry.

Crosses remind people of Jesus Christ. I was made aware of this when a businessman, seeing a small gold cross on the lapel of my jacket, asked me, "Why are you a believer in Christ?" I was glad for the opportunity to share my faith with him.

Jesus died on the cross for us, but we don't worship a dead Savior. Our Lord's body was taken down from the cross and placed in a tomb, and then on the third day He emerged in a glorified body.

The cross speaks to us of the total picture—our Lord's atoning death to pay the price for our sins, as well as His glorious resurrection to deliver us from the power of death. If it were not for what Christ did on the cross, we would all stand guilty before God and hopeless in the face of death. But through faith in Him, we receive the forgiveness of all our sins and the assurance that death cannot hold us.

Have you looked at the cross and placed your trust in the One who died there? It's the only sure and perfect remedy for guilt and fear.

—Herb VanderLugt

1 CORINTHIANS 15:3—
Christ died for our sins according to the Scriptures.

Read today's *Our Daily Bread* at **odb.org**

LEADER'S and USER'S GUIDE

Overview of Lessons: In His Presence

STUDY	TOPIC	BIBLE TEXT	READING	QUESTIONS
1	Introduction: The Life of One Soldier	2 Timothy 2:1–4	pp. 6–9	pp. 10–11
2	A Centurion's Life	Luke 7:1–10	pp. 13–15	pp. 16–17
3	Centurions in the New Testament	Matthew 8:5–13	pp. 19–23	pp. 24–25
4	The Centurion at the Cross (Part 1)	Matthew 27:45–54	pp. 27–31	pp. 32–33
5	The Centurion at the Cross (Part 2)	Luke 23:44–48	pp. 35–39	pp. 40–41

Pulpit Sermon Series (for pastors and church leaders)

Although the Discovery Series Bible Study is primarily for personal and group study, pastors may want to use this material as the foundation for a series of messages on this important issue. The suggested topics and their corresponding texts from the Overview of Lessons above can be used as an outline for a sermon series.

DSBS User's Guide (for individuals and small groups)

Individuals—Personal Study

- Read the designated pages of the book.
- Carefully consider the study questions, and write out answers for each.

Small Groups—Bible-Study Discussion

- To maximize the value of the time spent together, each member should do the lesson work prior to the group meeting.
- Recommended discussion time: 45 minutes.
- Engage the group in a discussion of the questions—seeking full participation from each member.

Note To The Reader

The publisher invites you to share your response to the message of this book by writing Discovery House, P.O. Box 3566, Grand Rapids, MI 49501, USA. For information about other Discovery House books, music, videos, or DVDs, contact us at the same address or call 1–800–653–8333. Find us on the Internet at **dhp.org** or send e-mail to **books@dhp.org**.